C PROGRAMMING LANGUAGE FOR BEGINNERS

A step by step guide to learn C programming and series

Will Norton

Legal & Disclaimer

The information contained in this book and its contents is not designed to replace or take the place of any form of medical or professional advice; and is not meant to replace the need for independent medical, financial, legal or other professional advice or services, as may be required. The content and information in this book has been provided for educational and entertainment purposes only.

The content and information contained in this book has been compiled from sources deemed reliable, and it is accurate to the best of the Author's knowledge, information and belief. However, the Author cannot guarantee its accuracy and validity and cannot be held liable for any errors and/or omissions. Further, changes are periodically made to this book as and when needed. Where appropriate and/or necessary, you must consult a professional (including but not limited to your doctor, attorney, financial advisor or such other professional advisor) before using any of the suggested remedies, techniques, or information in this book.

Upon using the contents and information contained in this book, you agree to hold harmless the Author from and against any damages, costs, and expenses, including any legal fees potentially resulting from the application of any of the information provided by this book. This disclaimer applies to any loss, damages or injury caused by the use and application, whether directly or indirectly, of any advice or information presented, whether for breach of contract, tort, negligence, personal injury, criminal intent, or under any other cause of action.

You agree to accept all risks of using the information presented inside this book.

You agree that by continuing to read this book, where appropriate and/or necessary, you shall consult a professional (including but not limited to your doctor, attorney, or financial advisor or such other advisor as needed) before using any of the suggested remedies, techniques, or information in this book

Table of Contents

Introduction

Programming has changed the world and is still ruling the technological industry with wonders achieved that is often difficult to imagine. Efficient programmers are scarce and industries are looking out for fresh talent. A lot of programmers in the initial stage of the technological revolution depended on badly written structured programming languages such as Pascal, Haskel, Cobalt etc.

They have serious issues with the syntactical structure and the way they define things. At this point, C has emerged as a logical and effective programming language that can achieve what it intended to. A lot of programmers at first found it very different from other languages they have learned. But as time passed on C has become programmers favorite and is still one of the most popular and beginners intended programming languages despite competition from other high-level programming languages such as Java and Python.

Even now, if you have any programming background from other traditional programming languages such as Java and Python, you will find it extremely hard to understand the essence of language and create complex programs by yourself in C language. A lot of beginners find C as an old programming language that is outdated now. However, it is false and C programming language is still a popular and important language to be learned if you are dealing with system programming use-cases such as compilers and embedded systems.

What will you learn from this book?

As mentioned beforehand, this book is a layman's introduction to the C programming language with the help of well-curated examples chosen by the book author. This book explains all the basic programming concepts in a much easier way to understand for beginners.

We hope that his book will serve as a good learning experience and a trigger to enjoy programming for our readers.

How to use this book?

Programming books are often theoretical and may make readers deviate easily. This is the reason why we wrote these simple programming books that will let you understand the topics in an easy way.

All we ask you is to enjoy the process of programming.

Use a compiler to practice all of the mentioned code in this book. Programming is best learned when you try to do things.

There a lot of books that teach C programming language in the market. Thanks for choosing to let you enlighten the importance of C language.

Let us start!

Chapter 1: What is the C language?

This book is a comprehensive introduction to C language with in-depth examples. It is often misunderstood that C has lost its popularity due to the entrance of modern programming languages such as Java and Python.

However, a lot of beginners don't understand that C is still extensively used to develop compilers and operating systems.

A lot of advanced programming concepts used in C language are still considered a pathway to understanding programming in a better way.

This chapter introduces various important characteristics of C language in detail. We recommend you to use an operating system of your choice to experiment with the programs introduced in this book.

Let us go!

History of C

It is mandatory to discuss the history of a programming language before starting to discuss its specific components, principles, and philosophy. In the 1970s when the programming industry was very small and when there were very few effective programming languages, C was invented in the Bell labs by Denis Ritchie. He developed C language to use it for the development of the UNIX operating system that Bell labs corporation is trying to build. Almost all the components of the UNIX system are extensively written using the C programming language. A lot of graphical user functionalities were also implemented with the help of the C language.

Luckily, UNIX has become very popular in the technological landscape and has given C its required popularity. With the initial success of C language, Denis Ritchie and Bell labs started to distribute C language within different operating systems. One of the famous operating systems that came equipped with C language in the old times is IBM PC. A lot of the computer-related industries started to implement their code while developing C programming applications. So, within a very little time, C has evolved into one of the most popular middle-level languages.

Even after 50 years after its invention, C is still considered one of the most important middle-level languages that the world has ever seen. It is still widely used to develop system programming applications and artificial intelligence applications that deal with hardware equipment such as Robotics and Electric cars.

Why is it so special?

First of all, understand that C language is considered bad for developing modern web and mobile applications.

There are several modern programming languages such as Java, Php to serve this purpose.

C language programming is exclusively used in real-world system applications where we need to work with the hardware at a low level.

Modern programming languages have very fewer libraries for this sort of implementation and practically very bad programmatical structure that can make them nearly impossible to effectively interact with the lower-level components of the hardware.

Whereas, C can interact with hardware components very effectively due to the syntactical structure and programmatical process flows it follows. This is the reason why still C is considered best to create new operating systems and compilers.

Features of C language

Even though C deals with low-level hardware resources it is often considered as a middle-level language because it integrates itself with various high-level programming language capabilities such as neat syntax and organizing structures.

C language is also known widely because it is used as an entry-level teaching resource in various universities such as Harvard, Stanford, and Princeton, etc.,

At the initial stages of the development of C language, it has become difficult for programmers to develop systematic updates for the programming language due to a lot of companies creating different libraries and features that can be added to the language. Due to this reason, International standard organization (ISO) started to declare individual library functions for the C programming language.

All the programmers are suggested to use this respective format for better results. You can find out the latest guidelines from the official C language website.

Here are some of the essential features of the C language:

1) Portable

C language is considered extremely portable and can be executed in any operating system. Previously, it is developed to be run on MS-DOS systems. But with the explosion of windows, Mac and Linux operating systems C has expanded its ability to support different operating systems. A lot of third-party software developers also have developed tens of compilers to run C language programs effectively.

2) Light

C language is often considered lighter than the other high-level programming languages that have occupied the mainstream industry today. Even C++, the successor of C language implements more lines of code than the C. The reason for the lightweight features of C is due to its effective syntax principles. A lot of modern programming languages such as Java, Scala are forced to use complex boiler code syntax to run applications on various platforms. C, on the other hand, uses simple and strict syntax that makes the language a light-weight programming entity.

3)Functional programming

The most important difference between C and other high-level languages is that it supports functional programming. It uses procedures to complete a task in a repetitive mode. Other high-level languages use the object-oriented paradigm to implement different features in the software. Functional programming is often considered effective to develop system-level applications.

However, with the latest updates, we can also implement the object-oriented paradigm in C language. After thorough checks we have done we are not completely satisfied with the object-oriented programming features that C language offers. We recommend you to learn Python or Java if you are keen to develop applications in the object-oriented paradigm. If you are comfortable with a simple, effective paradigm then we suggest you try procedural programming that C provides.

4) Extensible

One of the important features of the C language is that it can be expanded accordingly to utilize our purposes. A lot of space communication facilities such as NASA use this functionality to develop their libraries that can be used to interact with their hardware machines and rockets. This advantage of adding our own functions to the default library is very useful when you are developing your operating systems that are similar to Windows or Mac.

5)Usage of pointers

A pointer is an advanced feature that is available in C language to point out the hardware value of a variable. Pointers can be used to point to a memory location and can be used in the logical implementation of complex features in the program. Very few programming languages use pointers to represent storage location values. Even though having its disadvantages pointers are still a valuable source of resource to implement complex features in the software systems.

6)Huge library of functions

C provides a large library of system functions. All these functions serve a purpose and can be used for developing high-level system applications. We will be discussing different time functions and string manipulation functions in detail in the later chapters of this book.

Apart from these features, C language is also an open-source resource and is free to use.

With this, we have completed a brief and thorough introduction to the C language.

This chapter acts as an introduction to C language by experts' words.

In the next chapter, which is a continuation of the concepts explained here we will discuss various advantages and applications of C language in detail.

Let us go!

Chapter 2: Why C language is important?

The previous chapter is an ode to the importance and history of the C programming language in a comprehensive manner.

This chapter further expands the concepts that the previous chapter has introduced. We will in detail discuss different C versions that are available along with the applications and advantages of C programing language in detail.

This is a theoretical chapter that helps to place some pretty basic ideas in your mind which can help you when you are dealing with complex programming problems.

Follow along to know more about it!

Why is the C programming language important?

There are a lot of programming languages nowadays and all of them serve a significant purpose. This section of the chapter explains some of the reasonable arguments that prove that C language is better than those high-level modern programming languages. However, it is the programmer's own choice to choose the language that he is most comfortable with.

We are not denying that fact. We are just giving pretty basic arguments that prove that C language is the best for certain applications and mediums.

a) They are fast

The important advantage of C is it can deal directly with hardware resources. This advantage over other high-level languages makes C a fast processing language. A lot of other programming languages offer abundant extra features but they cannot beat the faster processing time that C offers.

b) It is portable

Portability is one of the main reasons for the initial success of C. Back in those days, assembly languages have made portability a distant difficulty and often forced programmers to create multiple versions of code to deploy on different devices. However, C started to offer advanced portability customizations that can help us run the program code on any platform with the help of a supportive compiler. You need not worry about your software not running on different operating systems anyone by using C as your primary development language.

c) Modularity

C language offers you to store the snippets of your code in the form of modular entities. These are like user made functions that can be imported whenever they are needed. These are more related to packages in Java programming language. Modularity's are extensible and can solve a lot of problems that programmers are facing.

d) A statically typed language

There is a lot of argument in programming circles between static and dynamic typed languages related to which is effective. The difference between dynamic and statically typed languages is that during compile time, statically typed languages show errors in a much faster significance. C is a statically typed language and performs at a faster rate due to this feature. However, we don't deny the fact that dynamically typed languages provide much better security features during the compilation process.

e) A learning resource

C language apart from holding a lot of advantages can help you understand programming in depth. A lot of modern programming languages are dynamic and will not provide you a way to learn and adapt the programming philosophy that paved a path for a technological revolution. However, C, on the other hand, provides a lot of significant information that can help you understand the working process of computers and programming.

This is the sole reason why C is extensively used as a primary programming language for various graduate courses in topmost universities.

f) Important to understand other languages

C is a learning pathway to understand different programming languages such as Python, C++, and C#. A lot of compilers, interpreters and IDE's of these famous programming languages are developed using C. Learning about C can help you understand the programmatical syntax structure of other high-level languages.

In the next section, we will in detail discuss some of the applications of the C programming language.

Follow along!

Applications of the C programming language

As said before, C is a system-level language that can be extensively used to develop system-level applications. Here are some of them.

a) To develop compilers

A lot of compiler technologies are built upon C. Compilers are an essential component that is necessary to run a software or an application. Also, compilers are required to understand the hardware architecture before compiling the program.

This is the reason why C programming language is highly adaptable for developing compilers and its add-on applications.

It can also be used to develop interpreters and assemblers.

b) To create operating systems

Operating systems are an easy interface that serves as a mediator between the user and the computer. A lot of operating systems use C as a primary language due to its extensibility and fast processing nature. Linux, a famous open-source operating system used C to develop its most important component kernel.

c) System-based applications

A lot of devices/applications that are linked with hardware resources use C to develop applications. For example, Tesla cars use C language to communicate between its components. Robotics, a future technology also focuses on much about complex C programming concepts.

What are some downsides?

Like other programming languages, C is also not perfect in some cases. This section is provided for you to understand what C cannot offer for the programmers.

a) It Doesn't support object-oriented paradigm

All of the programmers knew that the Object-oriented programming paradigm is one of the most important and widely used programming paradigms. However, C doesn't support OOP's and solely focuses on procedural programming with the help of functions. A lot of institutions, services use packaging structure to distribute files between their employees. So, due to the procedural nature of the C programming language, it is often not considered as a primary development language for projects that require a huge number of contributors.

b) Not everything can be done with C

C is not a multi-use language. It cannot be useful for web and mobile application development, unlike other high-level programming languages. For example, Java can be used to develop desktop, mobile and web applications. C is not a multi-purpose programming language but a programming language that serves its work best.

In the next section, we will discuss the available versions of the C programming language.

We will also provide a small tutorial to help you download the executable file of C language to install C dependencies and compiler in your system.

Follow along!

Versions of C

C language is usually available in 2 versions as explained below.

a) ANSI C

This is the old version of the C programming language that is used in Bell Labs to develop the UNIX operating system. This is often considered complex to learn and deal with.

You can download and install it from the official C language website.

b) ISO C

This is the modern C language package that is often used to create multi-purpose programming applications. It is extensible and light-weight. You can directly download it from the official website to start using it.

Installing C in Windows

Step 1:

Programmers usually use the GCC compiler to create C programming applications. To install the GCC compiler you need to first download few dependencies that are necessary to install it. First of all, download Cygwin from its official website. Install it in the default folder of your choice. Carefully download the correct version of Cygwin that is compatible with your windows operating system.

Step 2;

After installing Cygwin, you need to download GCC packages from its applications. These are essential to run the GCC compiler

Step 3:

In the last step, download the GCC compiler and change the environment variables to make the compiler work without any flaws. We recommend you to constantly update the compiler for accessing latest features

Installation in Linux:

To install a C compiler in Linux you need to use the pip package manager.

Here is the format:

pip install GCC

After downloading the GCC compiler, Linux kernel will check for the dependencies and will automatically download all of those resources for you. You can use the vim text editor to create code and save them to execute in the terminal interface.

Use the same procedure as windows, to download the GCC compiler for Mac operating system.

You can also download several IDE's and install them to use them with fewer memory resources. A lot of this software is available for all the famous operating systems.

With this, we have completed a brief introduction to the advantage of the C programming language. In the next chapter, we will start learning about the importance of the program in detail. Follow along!

Chapter 3: What is a Program?

From the 1950s computers have slowly occupied and lead the technological revolution. At the initial stages, it is considered extremely difficult to just do numerical calculations using first-generation computers.

Magnetic cards are used as input and output devices and they almost occupied a whole room. However, with time computer scientists have made this problem go away. Nowadays, we can find computers in the size of wrists with gigabytes of memory.

The success of computers is mainly due to programs that are used to make software.

Programming languages are developed to create meaningful programs. In this chapter, we will in detail discuss the importance of programs and how they work.

Let us go!

What is programming?

Computers are a lot different from humans.

They are not neurally active and doesn't consist of any emotions that humans possess. Computers mostly rely on instructions.

The only reason why computers have become better than humans is that they do tasks effectively without wasting any time. However, we can consider computers as dumb machines. If they are not provided with a solution to the problem beforehand, they can't solve it. Even after twenty years of tremendous research robotics is not a successful field because it is difficult to make machines that take decisions by themselves.

In the early stages of computer development, people used to use instruction sets to complete tasks. These instructions sets are allowed to use only for scientific and military purposes.

Several multinational companies started to experiment with their employees to create a whole new way to pass instructions to computers. All dreamt of an easy way to make things work out.

After a few years with great research, computer scientists introduced the concept of programming to the technological world with the help of programming languages. Programming languages provide a set of defined libraries that can help you to create programs.

Programs are considered as an analytical representation of algorithms and the definite task of creating valid programs that can be understood by a machine is known as programming.

In the next section, we will start discussing a program on a much deeper level.

What is a Program?

Programming languages use Programs to give varied instructions to the computing machines. From a mathematical perspective, the process of giving step-by-step instructions is called an algorithm.

A lot of statistical concepts in mathematics too use algorithms to solve a problem. An algorithm is not only a step-by-step procedure but a way that is proven to be effective.

In programming, we use programs to create a logical instruction that can make us solve a specific problem as quickly and effectively as possible.

Experienced programmers try to create programs that are in less code length and which consumes fewer resources. It is not only important to create a working code, but it is also important to create code that is feasible and which effectively understands the resources that are available to it.

What is the difference between Algorithm & program?

Algorithm and program are closely interlinked. When a programmer is trying to solve a problem, he first finds a logical and provable way to complete it.

He monitors the inputs and outputs that are available and creates a step-by-step procedure to solve it.

This is called an algorithm from a theoretical basis.

However, computers can't understand human language. They use the binary system to understand instructions.

This is the reason why we need to represent our algorithm in a way such that computers can understand.

This process is technically known as programming. Programming uses a set of programs to make the computer understand what needs to be done.

What are the programming languages?

When the concept of programming is introduced the scientific and computing community has overwhelmed. They started developing a lot of instruction sets and started developing programs with them.

However, just after a few projects programmers and computing scientists understood that there needs to be a specific regular platform to create programs. It is not feasible to use each other's instruction sets to create meaningful software.

So, they worked hard to develop programming languages that can maintain and provide a lot of libraries for their usage. Programming languages like ABC, Pascal are developed and people started using them for developing programs. All these distinct programming libraries are enhanced and named as programming languages. They are also called as high-level languages and remember that they are only used to make it easy for humans to communicate with computers.

We always need a compiler to let computers understand the program.

You will learn about the programming process in detail in the next chapter.

How programs can be written?

Programs are usually written in an operating system. For example, Windows is an operating system. Traditionally programmers used to use a text editor and command-line tools to write and run a program. But nowadays, a lot of programmers use IDE (Integrated development environments) to develop and debug programs. If you are working for an open-source project then you must have good knowledge about Git-based programs such as GitHub to access and contribute to the projects.

Here are some of the tools that can be used to develop C programming applications.

1) NetBeans IDE

NetBeans is a famous IDE that is often used by C language programmers to develop console applications. It has a good supportive development team that updates relevant features once in a while.

Compile-time is also very smooth and can help you create large applications with less RAM.

2) Code blocks

Code blocks is a multi-purpose ide that can be used to create programming applications. It is commonly used to develop C++ programs. However, you can use a simple tweak to start developing C language applications using it.

C programming provides a smart coding facility where you can easily highlight the relevant code.

3) Sublime text

Sublime text is not a usual IDE but a beautiful text editor that provides a lot of plugins to improve your productivity while programming. It also looks beautiful and is available in both free and premium versions.

4) Eclipse

Eclipse is an Integrated development environment that is usually used to develop java applications and android apps. However, Eclipse is also well versed with C addons to develop complex applications.

We recommend you to try Eclipse if you are trying to develop compiler software with C. Eclipse provides a linter to constantly check C syntax.

With this, we have completed a chapter that explains in-depth about a program.

In the next chapter, we will use certain programming concepts to understand the programming process.

Let us dive into it!

Chapter 4: What is a Programming process?

To understand C programming in depth it is important to learn about the default programming process in detail. Just like every other technological advancement, programming languages too follow a strictly adhered guideline system to make things work in the way they are intended to. In the previous chapter, we discussed in detail the basic structure of a program.

In this chapter, we will help you to understand the basic process of programming languages and programs itself.

This is a theoretical chapter and will introduce some of the historical concepts related to programming to make you aware of various instances.

Let us go!

In the previous chapter, we got a good layman understanding of the program. Programs are used to make computers understand what we are saying.

As said before, it is difficult to make computers understand the programs by themselves. So, computer scientists started to create programs that can be compiled and converted into machine language.

All the programs are compiled, interpreted before running the program.

This task is done by interpreters and compilers.

In the next section, we will talk about the programming process that happens when a program is compiled.

Programming process

Before trying to knowing about the complete programming process it is essential to know about assembly languages. Assembly languages are used extensively before the invention of programming languages.

Assembly languages provided programmers to deal with computers on a higher level. Before assembly languages, computer programmers used to remember binary sequences to complete very simple tasks. Even for a simple multiplication, it used to take minutes for the first-generation computers. Tedious, isn't it?

However, with the entrance of assembly languages, things became better. Assembly languages use a certain defined location or defined names to perform operations. So, to create applications programmers used to create assembled code which can be understood by an assembler to provide results. Eventually, though usage of assembly languages became troublesome for the programmers.

The failure of assembly languages is considered mostly because of its non-portability.

The assembled programming code can be only run in the machines that support the instruction set.

After the development of FORTRAN programmers understood the powerful capabilities that programming languages possess. Programming languages are machine-dependent and can be run on any system.

All we need to have is a compiler that can understand and interpret the instructions we are giving.

In the next section, we will in detail discuss the working procedure and philosophy of compilers.

What is a Compiler?

A compiler is a piece of computing component that lexically analyzes the programming code you have written and analyzes it to provide results.

Compilers are essential to run the programs that are created.

Compilers will also help you to understand the syntactical errors that you have performed.

What are the essentials to be remembered?

1) Always remember that the file name is necessary to help your compilers understand whether they are dealing with the right file or not. C++ compilers cannot understand C programming code and vice versa. Compilers are complex software programs that only work with the programming languages they are intended to work upon.

For example, you can't create iOS applications using Eclipse because Eclipse cannot compile iOS applications.

For, a C Program remember that files should consist of .C file format.

You can use a text editor such as vi text editor or sublime text editor to create program files.

2) The compilation process is started or enabled using a set of instructions. Command-line tools use certain syntactical commands to start the compilation process whereas Integrate development environments such as NetBeans use graphical user interfaces to start the compilation process.

Here is the format for the command line:

GCC sample.c

When this particular format is entered in the command line the compilation process will initiate and will show the results if there are no errors. If there are errors, they will be displayed along with the line number.

Process of compiling programs

The compilation is a complex process and involves different stages.

The compilation procedure will not continue further if it deals with any errors or warnings in the process.

Let us take a look into it.

Stage 1: Checking semantic nature

In the first stage, compilers check every component of the program using top to down basis. It checks whether or not the component is following the lexical syntax of the programming language. If everything is right the programming process will proceed to the next stage. However, if errors are encountered due to wrong syntactical structures such as wrong parenthesis statements or missing braces the program will abort and the compilation errors with possible reasons will be displayed on the screen.

Step 2: To assembly language instructions

In this stage, all the processed programming code will be analyzed and converted into assembly language code to be understood by the computing machine. All compilers provide different instruction sets to make this procedure complete fastly. This procedure is essential because an assembler is the only component taht is authorized to convert programming syntax into object code.

Step 3: Linking the object code

In the previous stage of the compilation process, we have generated an object code that can be understood by any computer. In this stage, we need to link the generated object code to any programs that are necessary to run the program. For example, consider packages and libraries that are essential to run the software. Linkage of programs is also known as building. When the object codes are linked you can obtain an executable file that can be opened to run the program. However, a lot of compilers automatically display this executable file as a result.

Step 4: Loading the program

In the last stage, all we need to do is enter the syntactical format that can help us run the program on the screen. For the C programming language, you need to enter a.out to run the program.

What happens after the compilation?

After the compilation process is completed the output will be displayed. If there are any instances where the input values should be entered the program will stop executing and will wait for the input values.

Programs will also respond to events such as mouse clicks. You can also use the debugging feature provided to change any lines of the code and execute the program all over again.

With this, we have completed a brief chapter that explains the programming process that is involved when a program is compiled.

In the next chapter, we will write our first C program and introduce a lot of essential and basic C concepts.

Follow along!

Chapter 5: Writing your first C program

Programming is learned in a better way when combined with examples that explain the syntax structure and process control that the programming language uses.

This chapter is a comprehensive one where we provide a C language example and explore the components of it in detail. Remember that, a lot of the concepts explained in this chapter will be further discussed in detail in the later chapters of this book.

For now, understand the specifics of C programming language with an example.

Follow along!

First C program

```
#include<stdio.h>
// Here, you should enter the main program
int (main {Enter the argument here})
{
  printf( " Christmas is coming soon')
// You can enter the return keyword here if needed
  return value;
}
```

Now, in this section, we will explain about the different components that are mentioned in detail.

Note: Remember that in C language there is no difference between upper- and lower-case letters. Also, whitespaces are allowed and you can start the program from any position on the line. However, it is recommended to follow design guidelines to create a readable programming code. Always follow the guidelines that are designated by the International standards organization (ISO).

1) #include <stdio.h>

This is an easy way to import a library and use the functions that are present in it in the program. It is mandatory to include <stdio.h> in every C program because it imports the major input and output functions such as printf and scanf. This is the format you need to use whenever you import a library to be used on the program code.

For example, #include <math.h> imports all the system math functions and #include<time.h> includes all the system time functions. These are also called as preprocessors in the programming terminology.

2) int main(void)

Here, the main is the program execution point that is often considered as an initial point for compilers. When a C program is compiled, the compiler first checks the code that is present between the braces of the main function. Here int represents the return type it is accustomed to. Also, remember that the void represents that the main function has no parameters. It is important to follow the instructions so that you won't mess up any logical code in the main function.

3) printf(" Christmas is coming soon')

Here printf is the system output function that can print out the values that are present in between the quotation marks on your screen. You can also use scanf to scan the input values. These are called input and output statements in the C programming language. When the program is compiled " Christmas is coming soon" will be displayed on the screen as an output.

4) return value

This is a statement that describes the return value that the main function produces. Usually, it is void or sometimes present in the null format. Return is an important functionality provided by the C programming language that can help us to maintain the resources effectively.

With this, we have explained in detail all the important components that are present in the first program we have discussed.

Compiling and Running the program

In this section, we will talk about the compilation commands for any C language file.

We will also provide instructions to help you run a program without any runtime errors.

Compiling a program

It is important to remember the file name and use the following format in the command line.

Always, make sure that you are in the same directory in the terminal as of the file location

$ GCC {Name of the program file}

When this format is entered on the terminal, it will take some time to compile the program. If there are no errors shown then the program is said to be compiled successfully.

However, if errors occur then you can't run the program unless they are cleared off.

Errors are usually displayed with the line number for easier understanding.

The program will not proceed further unless the errors or cleared off.

Running a Program

After compiling the program, it is now time to run the program using the command-line instructions.

Advanced programming environments such as NetBeans automatically run the programs after compilation is completed.

However, in the command-line interface, you need to enter the following command for running the program.

a.out

After entering the following command your program is completely ready to be run by the command-line interface. You can now enter your program name to display the result.

Here is the command:

$example.c

Here is the output:

Christmas is coming soon

Comments

In the above example program, you might have observed some of the remarks in the program followed by the "//" symbol. These are called comments in a programming language.

Comments are usually used to help programmers who are working in big projects to understand the declaration of variables and the logical algorithms used.

Comments are also an easy way to maintain coherence between the programmers involving in the programming project.

Comments are often considered as a good programming practice and we suggest you use comments while writing your programming code in C language.

C programming language usually provides two types of comments:

a) //

These comments are usually used in the middle of the programs. They are used for providing remarks for the program.

Function and variable declaration are the most common places where these comments (also called as single-line comments) are used.

b)/*.... */

These are called as multi-line comments and are often used at the beginning or end of the programs.

They are used to provide a detail explanation about the programming logic that has been used while writing the program.

They are also used at the beginning of the programs to explain the system libraries or third-party that have been imported for a particular program

For example, a lot of machine learning algorithms developed using C provides a detailed algorithm explanation to the program in the form of multi-line comments.

Variables

Variables are a way to store values and use them repeatedly whenever needed. We will in detail explain variables in the further chapters. But for now, it is recommended to watch out this example to help you understand how variables are declared in the C language.

For now, do not worry about the syntax because we will deal with in detail in the upcoming chapters of this book.

Here is the programming code:

```
#include<math.h>
main()
{
  variable1 = 23;
  variable2 = 45;
  variable3 = variable1+variable2;
  printf(" Print first number as %i/n",variable1)
  printf(" Print first number as %i/n",variable2)
  printf(" Print first number as %i/n",variable3)
}
```

The output will be :

Print first number as 23

Print second number as 45

Print third number as 68

Explanation:

In this program variable1, variable2 and variable 3 are programs that can store a value. The C programming language automatically determines that it is an integer value while taking the input. However, while displaying the print statement you might have observed that it requires parameters. %n is used to declare an integer output statement.

Here we have used assignment operators to declare variables and arithmetic operators to combine or add variables.

 In the next chapters, we will discuss important C operations in detail.

New lines

In the previous program, you might have observed '/n' in the programming code. This is usually used to print a new line in the result.

Here is a program:

```
#include<math.h>

main()

{

  variable1 = 67;

   variable2 = 78;

   variable3 = variable1+variable2;

    printf(" Print first number as %i/n /n %i /n ................. ",variable1)

}
```

The result will be:

Print first number as 67

67

....

With this, we have completed a brief introduction to the first C program written in this book.

In the next chapters, we will start an in-depth discussion about various important C programming language concepts.

Let us go!

Chapter 6: Functions

C is a procedural programming language that adversely uses functions to complete tasks. Unlike modern programming languages such as Java which uses classes and objects to create instances, you need to use functions to create varied instances.

Functions are usually determined as reusable code.

They are first implemented for using mathematical calculations in the 13th century.

In this chapter, we will in detail describe functions in the C programming language. We suggest you create your own programs to better understand functions.

Let us go!

What is a function?

Functions are generally used in the mathematical operations to repeat a calculation or set of expressions. Computer programming languages adopted these functional concepts to create and maintain certain defined instructions.

A lot of programming languages provide libraries that can be imported when they want to be used.

For example, in C programming language to use printf and scanf notations you need to import studio.h. This is because printf and scanf are standard input, output functions.

These are also called as system functions.

You can also use your own defined functions which are programmatically known as user-defined functions by importing them.

From a programming perspective, the function is a collection of logical and lexically correct statements that can be used for developing applications. Also, it is important to say that it is mandatory to have at least one function in the program.

Main is the default function.

Why functions are used?

Imagine programming with a lot of static code that does the same task. It is not feasible and consumes a lot of time for the programmers.

This is the reason why functions are used to regulate the large code and maintain equity in the program.

With the help of functions, we can divide the code into many modules and can easily check them with any available debugger. Functions are also to organize and maintain, unlike complex static code that can go on for an infinite distance.

For example, if you want to create a stock investor program in the normal programming instance you need to create static input and output for every option that is displayed on the interface.

However, in procedural programming with the help of functions, you can create options or menu instances that can be used whenever needed.

Advantages of functions

1) Easy

It is easy to maintain and debug the code when functions are present. You can't or it is practically not possible to develop complex code without functions. They are the actual building blocks of the c programming language and will always be. They are easy to create if you understand their basic implementation procedure.

2) Pathway to modules

Modules are an important component in the programming language. They categorize the language and divides or organizes meaningful code in one place. Functions are the basic nature of modules. If you learn about functions you can easily understand the complexity of modules. After learning about higher-order functions in-depth you will understand the importance of modules in a programming language.

3) Debugging

Debugging is a process where the programmers check the programming code continuously and change the affected program code if they find any bugs. Bugs can be used for exploitation purposes by hackers. When effective functions are written it is easy to just change their logic during the debugging process. In this way, we will not encounter any dangerous errors that may compromise the system.

4) Save time

With functions, you will save a lot of time during the programming process. This process is called as code optimization.

Types of functions

Every programming language provides a different type of default system functions. For example, you can use mathematical and time functions in C language from the default libraries. Users can also create functions with new parameters and logical statements.

These functions are called as user-made functions.

In the next section, we will explain about user-made functions and library functions in detail.

Follow along!

a) library functions

They are already pre-linked with the C compiler that they downloaded.

All the functions are stored in the default c folder and can be imported whenever needed. Printf, scanf are some of the famous predefined functions in the C programming language.

The merits of predefined functions are there is no need to specifically call them during the programming process. Also, they are fast because they are already linked to the compilers. However, remember that they are limited by the functionality they can offer and they cannot be extended by any means.

Also, no one can edit or change the default functions that the C programming provides unlike user made functions.

b) User-made functions

These are the functions that are created by the programmer. For creating functions, you need to follow certain guidelines that the C programming language provides. You need to first define functions and call them whenever needed.

In the next section, we will discuss the function declaration in detail.

Follow along!

How to define a function?

First of all, remember that functions have a unique name and reserved keywords cannot be used as function names.

Here is the format:

Datatype name (//Enter parameters here)

{

  // Enter function logic here

}

Here, a datatype is the return value of the function you are trying to create. For example, if a function returns negative decimal values you need to declare float variables as the data type.

In the next step, you need to enter a valid function name with parameters.

What is a parameter in the function?

To say in layman terms parameters are similar to variables but for functions. Each of the parameters is individually declared with a data type.

Only variables declared in the parameters can be used in the body of the function. If there are any misspells while creating or calling parameters of the function you will encounter run time errors.

At the last step, you need to create logical expressions and statements in the function body. In the function body, you cannot use variables or literals that are not declared before. So, make sure that all the specifiers are included before you start creating logical operations, conditionals, and loops in the function body.

How to call a function?

A function is useless if it cannot be used. Programming doesn't allow usage of functions just by their names due to various potential errors. You need to follow certain rules to call a function in the C programming language.

Here is the format:

Datatype function (// Enter the parameters here)

sample = function (//Enter the parameters here)

Here, the data type represents the type of return value you are expecting. Sample represents a variable name. A function can be called only if the variables are declared with a global specifier.

In the next section, we will in detail discuss function arguments.

Follow along!

What are the function arguments?

Arguments are the values that functions take in the parameter part of the function. You can create functions without arguments too.

There are some varied differences between functions with arguments and without arguments which we will be discussing now in detail.

Functions with arguments

If a function has arguments there is no need to declare variables again in the function body. When function arguments are declared you need to call the functions with arguments. If certain arguments are not shown while calling a function then it will end up with a syntax error.

For example:

function (int x, int y)

Here is a function with two arguments x and y. Here x and y are both of int data type. If you are calling this function in the middle of the program you need to use the below format.

function (3,4)

If you leave the arguments without any values you will not further proceed with the compilation process.

For example,

function (3)

Output:

The syntax is not complete

Functions without arguments

If functions are not declared or enclosed with arguments, they need to be called using a value or reference.

These functions are especially used while creating complex system learning applications.

They don't consist of any parameters but use variables as a way to expand the logical equivalence to the function statements and expressions.

Call by Value

When call by value argument instance is used you cannot change the parameter value again. T

his functionality is used especially when there is a necessity of using constant literal values in the function body.

Here is a program:

```
#include<stdio.h>
void sample (float first, float second)
{
 double result;
 result=first;
 first=second;
 second=first;
}
main ()
{
 float first=100, second=200;
 result (first, second); // passing value to function
 // This is an example to calling a function using a value
```

}

In this program, the function result is called using the value. This is an easy way to declare functions and use them.

In the next section, we will explain another advanced way to call function.

Call by reference

Usually, when a variable or literal is declared they are stored in a memory location. Memory locations can be used to modify or alternate statements and expressions.

You can easily know about your reference storage value using the pointers in the C programming language.

When some advanced functions are used, it becomes a necessity to call the function values using reference points. The advantage of this feature is function value changes everywhere in the program when a reference pointer is used.

Here is a program:

```
#include<stdio.h>
void sample (float first, float second)
{
 double result;
 result=first;
 first=second;
 second=first;
}
main ()
{
 result (&first, &second); // passing value to function by a reference
```

// This is an example to calling a function using a reference

}

In the above program, we use a function that calls the arguments with the help of reference values. In the next section, we will discuss recursion in detail.

Beginners are encouraged to learn about different system library functions too on their own. In the further chapters, we will discuss various string and time manipulative functions in detail.

For now, let us look at an example that helps you understand the essence of recursive programming in C.

Recursive functions

Recursive functions are used to decrease the code length of the complex problems such as sorting algorithms for an example. Creating a recursive function is difficult because it involves complex logical expressions. However, they are famous and popular in programming circles because they can reduce the load on the programing resources with their faster functional calling abilities.

In layman terms, Recursion is a function that repeats by itself. That is, it uses its own arguments as functional parameters.

Recursive functions are usually used in the creation and implementation of advanced data structures such as trees, graphs, and lists.

For your better understanding of the topic in this chapter, we will implement factorial using a recursive function. Follow along!

Here is the program:

```c
// Enter the libraries here
#include <stdio.h>
// Main function logic
main ()
{
  long int variable;
 for (variable=0; variable++;variable>11)
 {
   // We only display factorial upto 10 numbers
   /* You can change the variable limit if needed */
   print( %n, factorial)
   // Enter the return value here
 // Factorial recursive logic begins from here
 long int factorial(//Enter parameters here)
 {
  if (variable == 0 )
    factorail == 0
  else
    factorail = result * (result-1)
 }
return factorial;
}
```

Explanation:

In the above program, factorial is calculated by a recursive function that calls by itself. First of all, we create two global variables, result, and factorial in the body of the function. Result is a temporary variable that holds the values during the functional process.

Factorial is a variable that holds the end value and prints on the screen. They both use recursive logic to implement a factorial execution process in this program.

We use a conditional and loop statement constantly to check whether are not the limit of factorial is crossed. If 10 numbers are completed, the function will stop recusing itself.

We also used long, a program specifier for the integer values to allocate sufficient resources during the recursive process.

Exercise:

Try to create a recursive function for checking whether two numbers are prime or not.

Procedural programming in the C language

As said before, C is a procedural programming language that relies completely on functions to complete tasks.

The major advantage of procedural programming is they can be used to create a new set of programs from the old programs.

Object-oriented paradigm inspired programming languages such as Java consist of whole new instances and entities which can be difficult to maintain.

Procedural programming can be completely achieved only when you can use functions, identifiers, and logical expressions combined to create efficient programs. Procedural programming has its demerits too. It is not possible to create a machine learning and artificial intelligence applications with the C programming language because they cannot create automatic functions.

With this, we have completed a brief introduction to functions.

In the next section of this book, we will in depth discuss various advanced C programming features such as arrays, structures, and pointers.

For now, we suggest you look at some of the open-sourced GitHub projects to understand the usage of functions in-depth.

In the immediate next chapter, we will discuss various basic operations C programming language can perform.

Let us go!

Chapter 7: Operations

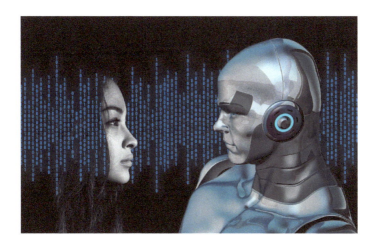

The previous chapter is a dive into the procedural philosophy of C programming language.

Creating functions and using pre-built system functions is the most important task that the C language does.

In this chapter, we will start discussing different C operators and operations that are essential for creating effective programs.

This chapter is explained from a programmatical perspective and consists of a lot of examples.

We suggest you open a compiler and experiment with the code that we present here.

Always remember that programming can be mastered only with practice.

Let us dive into the world of C programming operations!

What are the operations?

To explain in simple terms, operations are the replica of mathematical expressions in the programming languages. Usually, when we do a mathematical problem, we define constants and use functions to solve them using different mathematical applications.

In the same way, programming languages use different operators to achieve a lexical significance related to the mathematical application.

Mathematical operations

First of all, we will start with simple mathematical operators such as addition and subtraction.

Computing is based upon regular mathematical calculations and is mandatory to make programs work effectively.

To conduct mathematical operations with precision and effectiveness we use programming operators in C language.

a) Addition

The addition is usually done with the help of the '+' operator. Using this operator, you can add two variables or literals. You can also use this operator to join two strings.

Here is an example:

```
#include {The libraries needed]
main()
{
  variable1 = 32;
  variable2 = 12;
  variable3 = variable1 + variable2;
  // This is where we use a '+' operator
  printf(" This is the number %n",variable3)
}
```

Output:

This is the number 44

b) Subtraction

Subtraction is denoted by the operator '-'. Using this operator, you can remove or delete the strings and constants that are present. You can also use this operator for separating packages and libraries.

Here is an example:

#include {The libraries needed]

main()

{

  variable1 = 32;

  variable2 = 12;

  variable3 = variable1 - variable2;

  // This is where we use a '-' operator

  printf(" This is the number %n",variable3)

}

Output:

This is the number 20

c) Multiplication

This is the operator that can be used to multiply the variables and constants that are present. You can use this operator with strings to print continuous results. Multiplication operator is also effective for repetitive tasks. It is represented using the '*' operator.

Here is an example:

```
#include {The libraries needed]
main()
{
  variable1 = 32;
  variable2 = 12;
  variable3 = variable1 * variable2;
  // This is where we use a '*' operator
  printf(" This is the number %n",variable3)
}
```

Output:

This is the number 384

d) Division

This is the operator that is used to divide two variables or constants. It is usually represented by the ' / ' operator. We will also discuss the modulus operator that determines the remainder of the division in the later sections of this chapter.

Here is an example:

```
#include {The libraries needed]
main()
{
  variable1 = 32;
  variable2 = 12;
  variable3 = variable1 / variable2;
  // This is where we use a '/' operator
  printf(" This is the number %n",variable3)
}
```

Output:

This is the number 2

Operator precedence

It is also important to remember that the C programming language favors few operators above other operators. This is to resolve any conflicts or ambiguities in a mathematical expression. Usually, * and / are the highest priority operators followed by + and -.

It is important to remember the concept of operator precedence while dealing with a lot of associative code.

As said before, these are the basic operators that are available in the C programming language. C also offers several assignment and logical operators to help you create complex programs.

In the next section, we will start looking at operators in a much deeper sense.

Assignment operator

The assignment operator is used to declare or initiate any identifiers. For example, variables are initiated using the assignment operator.

Here is the format:

variablename = value;

Here '=' is called the assignment operator.

When an assignment operator is used usually the variable is initiated. The assignment operator can also be used to replace the values. Assignment operators turn statements into mathematical expressions.

They can also be used as mutually exclusive and inclusive statements. Assignment operators can be combined with '+' and '-' to create counter operators such as '+=' '-='.

These operators are usually used in producing logical expressions.

Comparison operators

These are the operators that can be used to produce logical equivalence statements. They can be used to compare to statements and provide an option to choose the programming flow.

These operators will be extensively used to develop conditional and loop statements.

a) Equal to operator (==)

This is the operator that is used to compare whether two statements or identifiers are equal or not.

Here is an example:

variable = 23;

varib = 46 ;

if (varfiable == varib)

printf(" this is good")

else

printf(" This is wrong")

Output:

This is wrong.

b) Not Equal to operator (!=)

This is the operator that is used to compare whether two statements or identifiers are not equal.

Here is an example:

variable = 23;

varib = 46 ;

if (varfiable != varib)

printf(" this is good")

else

printf(" This is wrong")

Output:

This is good

c) Greater than and less than operators

These are the operators that can be used to compare two identifiers based on their values. If the logical statement is correct than the value will be produced as a result.

Here is the program:

variable1> variable2

// This is called greater than operator

variable1< variable2

This is called less than operator

variable <= variable2

This is called less than or equal to operator

variable1 >= variable2

This is called greater than or equal to operator

Modulus operator

The modulus operator is considered to be one of the essential operators for programming languages. It just prints out the remainder as the result. However, this mathematical application can be used to regulate system expressions and develop effective system applications.

For example:

if (Var1 % var2)

printf(" This is great")

Logical operators

C language also provides logical operators to compare two statements from a purely logical perspective.

The famous logical operators are AND, OR and NOT.

We will explain them in detail in the next section. Follow along!

a) AND operator

This logical operator displays the result only when both the statements that are involved are true. If any one of them is not true then the program will not execute.

Here is the program code:

```
#include<math.h>

//This is used to import mathematical functions

main()

{

  int a=3;
```

```c
int b=6;
int c= a*b;
if( a == 3 AND b == 5)
{
   printf( " This is the correct statement")
}
else
   printf(" This is the wrong statement")
}
```

Output:

This is the wrong statement

In the above program, the second statement is displayed as a result because one of the two statements is not true.

b) OR operator

This is a logical operator that displays the result even if any one of them is true. If both statements are not true then the other statement will be executed as a result.

```c
#include<math.h>
//This is used to import mathematical functions
main()
{
   int a=3;
   int b=6;
   int c= a*b;
   if( a == 3 OR b == 5)
   {
      printf( " This is the correct statement")
```

```
    }
  else
     printf(" This is the wrong statement")
}
```

Output:

This is the correct statement

c) NOT operator

NOT operator is used to display when a statement is false. If not the other statement will be executed.

```
#include<math.h>
//This is used to import mathematical functions
main()
{
   int first=3;
   if( first == 3 NOT b == 5)
     printf(" This is the wrong statement")
}
```

Output:

This is the wrong statement

Conditional and Loop operations

a) Conditional

Conditional statements are used in the C programming language to make decisions. They are advanced components of C and can be used in nested structures too. They consist of an if and an else statement.

Here is the format:

if(condition)

{

   // Enter the statement

}

else

   // Enter the statement

Here is an example:

a=7;

if(a==3)

printf(" This is true")

else

printf("This is false)

Output:

This is false

b) Loop statements

Loop statements are used in C programming to do repetitive tasks. Here, we will use for loop to help you understand the impact of the looping operations.

Here is the format:

```
for(i=value;i++;variable)
{
  // Enter the statements
}
```

Here is an example:

```
int a=0;
for(i=0;i>10;i++)
{
  i =10;
  i++;
  printf(" The results: %d',a)
}
```

With this, we have completed a comprehensive chapter that explains to you about various operations that are available in the C.

In the next chapter, we will in detail discuss structures one of the most important components of C programming language.

Follow along!

Chapter 8: Structures

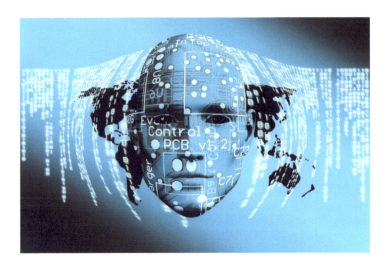

In programming languages, we often use interlinked variables to solve problems. C programming language provides structures as a basis to categorize interlinked entities while programming.

In object orient paradigm supported languages, classes are used to create a linkage between the variables. However, C is a procedural language that doesn't support classes.

With continuous development, C has found a way to counter this advantage of object-oriented programming languages using structures.

Structures do the same work as classes do but more effectively.

We will also provide various examples to help you understand the importance of structures.

Follow along!

Why is grouping necessary?

Usually, programming languages are with a large number of system functions. You can also create a lot of global and local variables during the creation of software.

When the programming complexity increases it makes things difficult to organize and maintain. So, to categorize variables and functions the concept of structures is introduced in the C programming language.

It serves an important purpose and can make programming effective.

In the next section, we will explain about the programmatical interpretation of structures in larger detail. Let us go!

What are the structures?

During the initial stages of C language development variables are first used to store values and functions to apply features on those values. However, with the increase in the data arrays are invented to store multiple values with a single entity name.

Arrays can be one-dimensional and two-dimensional and can store a lot of elements. The demerit of arrays is that all available elements in the arrays can be only of a single data type.

To counter this demerit in arrays, structures are developed. To make you understand in layman terms, structures are discrete programming components that can store variables of different data types. For example, you can create an int variable and a float variable at the same time using a structure.

To help you delve into the theoretical understanding of structures let us consider an example. Imagine a bookstore that requires a program to handle the book operations.

Here are some of the data types that can be used:

Bookname of string type

BookId of Integer type

Price of Integer type

Author name of string type

Using structures, you can create all these variables at once and can use them in multiple instances. All the variables that are created while a structure is represented as members of the structures.

You can define whether or not to use these members in the other parts of the programming code. There is a lot of customization in structures making it one of the most important components of C programming language.

To make things more interesting you can also use arrays and pointers during the structure creation.

You can also create a nested structure to further increase the effectiveness of the program.

In the next sections of this chapter, we will discuss all of these details about structures in detail.

Let us go!

How to define a structure?

The structure is a programming entity that holds different types of variables as explained before. C programing language uses certain varied distinctions to declare a structure.

Here is the format:

struct {Enter the name of the structure here}

While creating a structure, all you need to do is enter the 'struct' keyword along with the name you want to give it. After that, you need to create a body of the structure with defined variables using the format given below.

```
struct sample

{

   int number;

   char sex;

    int houseno;

    string name;

};
```

In the above program, the declared variables are called the members of the structure.

They can be used with access modifiers to make them global variables or not.

Always remember that you need to use a semicolon to end a structure.

If not, you will be shown a syntax error.

How to use structure variables in the main function?

Now, we need to know the way to use structure members in the main function. Whenever a structure is defined, they should be allowed to be used by another entity.

Here is the format:

main()

{

struct sample entity1,entity2;

}

Now, when the struct variables are declared both of them(i.e entity1 and entity2) can have each instance of the member that is present with the structure.

How to access these structure entities?

All you need to do is use the dot '.' symbol to make the declared variables in the main function access the members of the structure.

Here is the format:

entity1.name;

Use the above format to print out the elements present in a structure.

With this, we have discussed structures in brief. To learn about structures in much more depth we recommend you to look at the official documentation. In the next chapter, we will discuss in-depth the manipulation of strings. Follow along!

Chapter 9: Manipulation

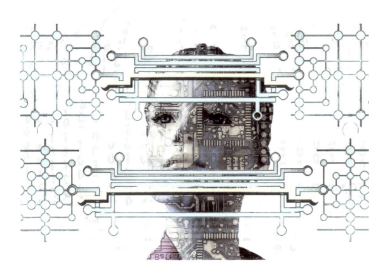

Strings are one of the most important and effective datatypes of the C programming language.

A lot of program user interfaces use strings to get implemented.

Strings can be used to store a lot of data. A lot of machine learning and system applications import data in the form of strings. Manipulations are a technique to control the strings data that we have access to. Strings can be manipulated to get reversed or divided according to our instructions. C language provides a library to implement the procedures of string manipulation.

In this chapter, we will discuss various system functions that can change the course of strings. Look at the examples we have provided in this chapter carefully and try to implement those system functions in your programs.

Let us go!

Why is Manipulation necessary?

Manipulation of strings is necessary because changing the strings manually is burdensome and time-consuming. Using the library functions, we can change an array of strings within no time

. Also, C programming language provides tens of system functions to manipulate strings which are often complex and difficult for the programmers to handle.

For example, A string can be reversed automatically using the reverse () function.

How Manipulations can be implemented?

First of all, to implement manipulations on the string data we possess we need to import the string library that holds a lot of manipulative functions.

Here is the format:

#include <string.h>

After importing the library, you can call the functions to the string variable or array present to look at the results. You can look at the C documentation to know about various string manipulative functions.

In this chapter, we will look at some of the most important string manipulative functions with examples.

Follow along!

Manipulative string functions

a) Concatenating two strings

Using this manipulative function, you can combine two strings that are present. We will provide an example to help you understand this function in detail.

Here is the program code:

```
// You need to import the string manipulation function library
#include<string.h>
main()
{
// Enter the first string
stringsample1 = " This is great";
// Enter the second string
stringsample2 = " This is awful"
// Now you need to enter the string concatenation function
string result = *strcat (stringsample1,stringsample2)
// Now print the result
printf(" Here is the result : result", %s)
}
```

Output:

Here is the result:

ThisisgreatThisisawful

You can find out from the result that the two strings have been concatenated.

b)Comparing two strings

This is a manipulative function where two strings are compared. The results will be in integer format where the negative number represents that the first string has more similarities than the second and the positive integer represent the latter. If 0 is displayed then it informs that the two strings are equal. We will give an example to help you understand this manipulative function in detail.

Here is the program code:

```
// You need to import the string manipulation function library
#include<string.h>
main()
{
// Enter the first string
stringsample1 = " Hello America";
// Enter the second string
stringsample2 = " Hello Newyork"
// Now you need to enter the string compare function
string result = *strcmp (stringsample1,stringsample2)
// Now print the result
printf(" Here is the result : result", %s)
}
```

Output:

Here is the result:

8

By the result, we understand that the string 2 differs from string 1 with 8 characters.

c) Copy strings

This manipulative function will help you to copy one string to another string. This is usually used in the advanced implementation of office programs.

Here is the program code:

```
// You need to import the string manipulation function library
#include<string.h>
main()
{
// Enter the first string
stringsample1 = " ";
// Enter the second string
stringsample2 = " This is copied"
// Now you need to enter the string copy function
string result = *strcpy (stringsample1,stringsample2)
// Now print the result
printf(" Here is the result : result", %s)
}
```

Output:

Here is the result:

This is copied

d) To upper case

With this string function, all the characters will be changed to upper case letters. Look at an example to understand it in a much better way.

Here is the program code:

```
// You need to import the string manipulation function library
#include<string.h>
main()
{
// Enter the first string
stringsample1 = " This is not easy";
// Now you need to enter the string upper case function
string result = struprcase(stringsample1)
// Now print the result
printf(" Here is the result : result", %s)
}
```

Output:

Here is the result:

THIS IS NOT EASY

e) To find the string length

With this, we can find the number of characters in the string. The string length will be displayed in the number format as a result.

Look at the below example to understand it in a better way.

Here is the program code:

```
// You need to import the string manipulation function library

#include<string.h>

main()

{

// Enter the first string

stringsample1 = " Hello America";

// Now you need to enter the string length function

string result = strlen(stringsample1)

// Now print the result

printf(" Here is the result : result", %s)

}
```

Output:

Here is the result:

11

f) To lowercase

This is a string manipulative function that can be used to display all the characters to lower case letters.

Here is the program code:

// You need to import the string manipulation function library

#include<string.h>

main()

{

// Enter the first string

stringsample1 = "This is great!";

// Now you need to enter the string lowercase function

string result = strlwr (stringsample1)

// Now print the result

printf(" Here is the result : result", %s)

}

Output:

Here is the result:

this is great

g) String error

The string error function is used to display error for a particular problem. This can be implemented easily as shown below.

Here is the program code:

```
// You need to import the string manipulation function library
#include<string.h>
main()
{
// Enter the first string
stringsample1 = " Hello America";
// Now you need to enter the string error function
string result = strerr (stringsample/0," You can't divide a string with 0")
// Now print the result
printf(" Here is the result : result", %s)
}
```

Output:

Here is the result:

You can't divide a string with 0

With this, we have completed a brief introduction to string manipulations in C programming language. In the next chapter, we will discuss constants in detail. Follow along!

Chapter 10: Constants

In programming languages, variables are used to store literal values. These literal values are usually called as constants in mathematical terms. Constants are important to give a certain value to the variable that you have created. Constant values can be easily replaced or manipulated with the help of functions.

Constants are also divided into different categories depending on the storage value. In this chapter, we will give a thorough explanation of constants with a lot of examples. Follow along to know more about it.

What are constants?

According to layman terms constant is a value that is fixed and holds a literal value in the canonical terms. Almost all programming languages deal with constants.

In a programmatical sense, they are called literals because they cannot be replaced unless a variable is changed.

In the next chapters of this book, we will discuss various data types that are declared when a variable is initiated or created.

For now, remember that data types are used to define constant values. The sole difference between literals and identifiers is that they cannot be changed.

Some of the famous constant values are integer constants, floating-point constants, and enumeration constants.

In the next section, we will comprehensively discuss them. Follow along!

Integer constants

An integer is a common way to define numbers in the programming languages.

In normal mathematics scenarios, there are usually different types of mathematical systems to denote numbers. For example, the decimal system is a mathematical number system. In the same way, programming languages can also determine various number systems and constants.

Integer constants can be normally represented in three systems in C programming language namely decimal, octal and hexadecimal.

Here are the examples:

3778

// This is a decimal number system

/* They usually represent numbers from 0 to 9 */

4664

// This is an octal representation

/* They only represent numbers from 0 to 7 */

0xdef

// This is a hexadecimal representation

Integer constants can be used in arithmetic and mathematical calculations. They can also be used in performing logical evaluations. A lot of hexadecimal notation is usually used to represent computer memory locations.

Floating-point constants

As explained before, integer constants cannot hold all the different types of mathematical representations that are available.

They are only created for storing simple numerical literals. Floating-point constants are much more advanced entities that can hold different mathematical constants such as exponential and negative.

Here are some of the examples:

3.24343

// This is a floating-point constant

3.894e

// This is an exponential constant

-445.3545

// This is a negative floating-point literal

Floating-point literals can be easily used to manipulate complex computer programs.

They can also be used to perform logical evaluations and operations.

Character literals

Characters are usually single letter arguments. They can be used for the smart processing of data in the program. However, C programming language has implemented character literals to create new lines and new tabs.

/n,/x are some of the examples of the character literals. Here is a good description of them.

1) /n

This is a character literal that can be used to create a new line in the program result.

2) /t

This is a character literal that can be used to create a new tab in the program result

Character literals are often used to determine newly created functions. They can also be used in the place of function arguments.

String literals

String literals are usual string data type entities that can hold a lot of continuous data. A lot of computer programs use string literals to input data.

Here is an example:

" This is a new world. This is the end of the world too"

// This is a string literal

104

How to define a constant?

Apart from using normal equivalent literals, you can also create constant literals that can be used at any part of the program just by calling the name of the constant.

Here is the format:

#define {Enter the identifier and constant value here}

For example:

#define Area=25metere

In the program, whenever Area is called in a function or using a template the constant will be sued.

There is also another way:

You can also use the constant keyword and the data type to give a literal value to the variable. This is used in a lot of system application libraries to start things in a better way.

const {Enter the data type} {Enter the value}

For example:

const int stupid = 64;

You can use the following constant and print results whenever needed using the %d notation.

These are some of the famous ways to define and create constants. In the next section, we will describe different types of constants based on storage values.

Specifiers

Constants in C programming language usually have specifiers to enhance the performance of the program. These specifiers will help you regulate the storage memory allocation.

For example, you can use long along with int data type to deal with larger values.

You can also use small with float literals to deal with less negative values.

Why specifiers are important?

Sometimes when we are dealing with programming code you can't understand how to allocate resources so that the programs will effectively.

For example, a buffer overflow execution error with constant literal values can make things difficult for the processor. So, when you are dealing with larger values it makes sense to predefine them to allocate sufficient resources for them.

In the same manner, mentioning specifiers can help the computer to understand that fewer resources are sufficient for the program. Specifiers increase program interactivity between the system allocations and resources.

Here are some of the examples:

long int first = 372737LL

small int second = 3

With this, we have completed a brief explanation about constants and literal values.

This is a comprehensive topic and we suggest you experiment with some of the code provided here on your compilers.

In the next chapter, we will start discussing Arrays in detail. Follow along!

Chapter 11: Arrays

Usually, in the programming languages, variables are used to store values. They are designated with the help of data types and can be used across functions, structures, and every other programming component.

Despite all the advantages variables possess they are quite useless when dealing with large data.

For dealing with larger data programming languages use structures called Arrays.

In this chapter, we will in detail discuss the importance of arrays along with its implementations and examples.

Follow along!

Why are Arrays necessary?

Arrays are a set of items that are ordered in a sequence. All the items can be easily pulled out whenever necessary by the program.

The usage of Arrays became familiar when programmers started to develop complex and large applications that deal with huge data. At the initial stages of computing, there was only a necessity of a few inputs and calculations. However, with the expansion and popularization of programming languages, people started to input large numbers of data.

For a few years, people used variables to do bulk operations. However, as data increased, they understood how difficult it is to organize and compare multi-data using variables.

To counter this problem Arrays are first introduced in the C language and since then Arrays are an essential component and a necessity to develop complex and large applications.

How to define an array?

Just like every other programming component arrays are required to define using a predefined format.

Arrays consist of index and subscript to easily maintain the set of values.

Here is the format for an array:

Arrayname = subscript[]

// This is the array designation

x[]

// This is the subscript of the file

[1]

// This is called index in terms of programming

For example:

example = sample[5]

Here 'example' is the array name and has a 5 set of values. Here the values are represented using the subscript.

For your better understanding, here are the set of variables that are enclosed in this array:

sample[0]

sample[1]

sample[2]

sample[3]

sample[4]

Here 0,1,2,3,4 are called the index of the array.

Note: Remember that the index of the array starts from 0 but not from 1.

A lot of people confuse with this simple mathematical notation while dealing with operations.

Advantages of Arrays

As explained before, arrays are extensively used to deal with high-level efficient programs. You can use them to determine or change the features of system-level software. Arrays are also easy to identify and can save a lot of programming resources.

Apart from being an efficient programming component arrays can be used in a lot of looping programs that deal with repetitive tasks.

Note:

In the subscript of the array bracket, you can also use mathematical expressions and statements.

For example, array = dude[integer/2]

How arrays manage memory?

Arrays use the stack principle to store data in the memory locations. If you want to add or delete an element from the arrays you can only do it at the end of an array.

Arrays are stored cumulatively and sequentially in the storage points.

For example, if the first element of the array is stored in 111a of the computer memory. Then the next four elements will be stored in the memory locations 111b,111c,111d.

When an array is created memory allocation is done at the beginning.

How to use arrays as counters?

Counter statements and operators are used to increase the data or variable literals exponentially. For example, you can multiply 100 times of a number using the counter statements. Arrays can also be used as counters in the C programming language.

We will use an example to help you understand the C language usage of arrays:

```
#include {enter the library here]

void ()

{

  int samplearray[10];

  for ( i=0; i++; samplearray)

  {

    scanf (" %n, " Use this")

    printf( " Enter the values")

    samplearray++;

  }

}
```

Here in this program, the counter values are automatically increased by using the output statements.

This program also uses Scanf to recognize the array index values. Look at the samplearray[] to understand arrays.

The index is automatically using the loop statements that are provided. Arrays used in this program make sus understand that arrays are variables that can store data with high precision.

In the next sections, we will learn about the initialization of variables and the multidimensional array's importance in detail.

Follow along!

Initializing arrays

Arrays are used as an easy way to store multiple values. All these values can be updated manually or automatically using default programs. Arrays can be initialized individually using the following format.

datatype arrayname[subscript] = {}

In the braces, you can enter the values of the arrays. The array subscript is counted with the order of the arrays inside the braces.

Here is an example:

int sample[5] = {3,4,5,,7,8}

Now, the arrays are initialized and hold a certain value. For example, sample[4] has a value of 8. This is an easy way to initialize variables. You can also use loop statements to automatically fill arrays while they were being used for functions.

Arrays can be initialized for any data type.

Characters and float data types are extensively used while initializing arrays.

All you need to change the data type value in the initialization format.

Another way to initialize:

You can use for loops to initialize arrays. It is often considered difficult to i individually enter the values for the array elements. So, if you already have data in a text file then you can use array system functions to scan and input the values in the array.

Here is the program:

```
for(i=0;i++;array)
{
  array[i];
  i+=;
  array[0] = array[0]+=1;
}
```

With this format, you can enter values easily into arrays. You can also initialize char arrays using the above format.

Constants with Arrays

You can use const identifiers to deal with variables that cannot change the array specifications. A lot of elements in the array remain empty and will not serve any purpose for the system resources.

Here is the code:

const array[] = {}

Multidimensional arrays

Multidimensional arrays are special programming components that can be used to create advanced data structures and matrix operations.

Here is the format:

arrayname[][]

The first value is called the row of the array and the second value is known as the column of the array.

When we multiply both values, we get the total number of elements present in the array.

Here is the code:

array[2][3]

Here, the number of elements is 6.

With this, we have completed a brief explanation about arrays.

In the next chapter, we will discuss time functions in detail. Follow along!

Chapter 12: Time Functions

C programming language provides various standard libraries that perform different actions. We have already discussed input, output and string manipulative functions. C programming also provides various standard mathematic functions.

In this chapter, we will discuss time and date functions that are quite essential for programmers. Time and date functions will be handy while creating programs that need automatic functioning according to the date and time.

For example, an alarm app needs to access standard time and date functions.

Try to look out at the examples and use them according to your convenience.

Follow along!

How to declare time functions?

As we are aware of the previous chapters, to import time and date functions we need to enter the preprocessing library at the starting of the code. Here, the library name is time.h.

Here is the format:

#include<time.h>

All the functions that are present in the time standard library use two types of format to represent time. In the first standard, time is the default in every region.

The time and date will be according to the Georgian calendar.

This format is automatically used by the C standard library whenever a library function is instantiated.

The second format is much more complex and deals with local time. It differs from region to region according to the location you are in.

This local time is also said to use day times saving functionality to give accurate results.

In the next section, we will in detail discuss the most important time manipulative functions with examples. Follow along!

Time and Date functions

a) Clock function

This is a standard time function that describes the time that the processor uses. The processing time is calculated right from the program that has been instantiated.

Here is the program:

#include <time.h>

// This is the standard time library that needs to be imported

main()

{

// Create a variable to store the result

float example;

result = clock_t (example);

// This is the clock function that prints out the processing time

printf(" Here is the result: %f', result)

// We print out the result of the time function

}

Output:

Here is the result:

4.34224 s

The output that has been displayed is the processing time for this particular program.

b) difftime

This is a complex manipulative function that can be used to find the difference between the two calendar times provided.

Here is the program:

#include <time.h>

// This is the standard time library that needs to be imported

main()

{

// Create a variable to store the result

float difference;

result = difftime (difference1,difference2);

// This is used to find the difference between two calendar times

printf(" Here is the result: %f", result)

// We print out the result of the time function

}

Output:

Here is the result:

12h32m32s

c) time function

By using this function, you can display the exact time at this moment. You can change the format of the time displayed using the spacebar option.

Here is the program:

#include <time.h>

// This is the standard time library that needs to be imported

main()

{

// Create a variable to store the result

float exacttime;

result = time(exacttime);

// This is used to display the exact time at present

printf(" Here is the result: %f', result)

// We print out the result of the time function

}

Output:

Here is the result:

12:23:21

d) asctime

The asctime is used to display the time in a different display format that is compatible with ASCII format.

Here is the program:

```
#include <time.h>

// This is the standard time library that needs to be imported

main()
{
// Create a variable to store the result

float format;

result = asci (format);

// This is used to display time in ASCII format

printf( " Here is the result: %f', result)

// We print out the result of the time function
}
```

Output:

Here is the result:

Sat Oct 22 03:11:34 2020

e) ctime

This will change the local time of your region to the default Georgian calendar that is used by the programming environment.

Here is the program:

#include <time.h>

// This is the standard time library that needs to be imported

main()

{

// Create a variable to store the result

float change;

result = ctime (change);

// This is the default georgian calendar time

printf(" Here is the result: %f', result)

// We print out the result of the time function

}

Output:

Here is the result:

22:12:23 changed

f) Local time

This will display according to the local time of your location. For example, PST time.

Here is the program:

#include <time.h>

// This is the standard time library that needs to be imported

main()

{

// Create a variable to store the result

float time;

result = local (time);

// This is used to display the local time

printf(" Here is the result: %f', result)

// We print out the result of the time function

}

Output:

Here is the result:

12:12:32

g) gmtime

This is used to display the default UTC according to the ISO conventions.

Here is the program:

#include <time.h>

// This is the standard time library that needs to be imported

main()

{

// Create a variable to store the result

float default;

result = gm (default);

// This is the clock function that displays UTC time

printf(" Here is the result: %f', result)

// We print out the result of the time function

}

Output:

Here is the result:

12:32:45

h) mktime

This format will display the week and month of the calendar in a good format.

Here is the program:

#include <time.h>

// This is the standard time library that needs to be imported

main()

{

// Create a variable to store the result

float calendar;

result = mktime (calendar);

// This prints out the calendar in a good format

printf(" Here is the result: %f', result)

// We print out the result of the time function

}

Output:

Here is the result:

JULY 12 2020 THURSDAY 22Hours:32Minutes: 23Second:32Milliseconds

With this, we have completed a comprehensive chapter that describes various time functions that are available in C programming language.

In the next chapter, we will discuss in detail about variables in depth.

Let us go!

Chapter 13: Variables

Variables are one of the important components of any programming language.

They store values and are often used in functions, structures, and templates. It is always recommended to learn about variables in depth before starting to create complex programs. I

n this chapter, we will discuss variables with various examples.

Follow along!

What are the variables?

It is important to understand the historical significance of memory management before understanding variables. Before the invention of programming languages, all the memory is managed using the binary sequences.

Everything is needed to be done in the hardcoded away. All of the significant memory locations are stored using a specific memory address in the computer.

However, with time these hardcoded methods are proven to be ineffective.

A lot of high-level programming languages started to use variables which are a symbolic representation of the memory locations.

How are the variables assigned?

First of all, remember that to create variables you need to define data types. These are also used for assigning literal constants. Data types are an easy way to distinguish the variables.

Why are data types necessary?

Imagine that you need to create a program that takes only characters as input values. It is not feasible to use strings that take up storage memory. Data types are used for faster memory processing and effective storage management. There are different types of data types such as integers, floating-point numbers and double. Data types can also be used to store pointers that store the variable address. We will learn about pointers in-depth in the upcoming chapters.

Rules for creating variables

Variables are defined using certain preconceived instructions. They are often started using an underscore. However, remember that variables are not case sensitive. so, both upper case and lower-case letters can be used to create variables.

Note: Reserved keywords cannot be used as the name of variables. There are more than 60 default reserved keywords in the C programming language that cannot be used as identifiers.

You can find out the reserved keyword list from the official website.

Tip:

Make variable names simple. It is not feasible to use complex long names to declare variables. You can, of course, do it but it is not a good programming practice.

Here are some of the good variable declaration examples:

ramdas

_Usa

Randis

Here are some of the bad variable declaration examples:

1sery

thisisalongvariablename

*gdhd

pointer

In the next section, we will in detail discuss data types that are essential for the variables.

a) Numbers

Numbers are the most important data entity that is used in programming. All the mathematical equations and algorithms require integral constants to solve the specific problem. C

 programming uses various data types to declare numerical variables.

i) int

This is the most common data variable that is used to declare numerical variables. int cannot store decimal values and is said to occupy till ten digits. It stores a few bytes of data whenever a variable is declared. While implementing the printing statements, %n can be used to print the variables with the int data type.

You can also use %x and %o to print the stored values in different formats such as octal and hexadecimal. Usually, int data type occupies 32 bytes of storage in the memory.

ii) float

Floating-point numbers are used to represent decimal and scientific notations. It can occupy up to 64 digits and can be used while developing complex scientific applications. A lot of exponential problems and modulus calculations can be done with the help of floating-point literal.

When printing the output statements %f is used as a notation.

iii) double

Double is the advanced expansion of floating-point literals. In double both negative and positive decimal notations can be used. They can extend up to 128 digits. You can use %f or % e to print the double literals as an output.

b) Characters

After numbers, the most important data types should be of characters and strings. Almost all applications rely on characters to communicate with the users. Here are the character datatypes that C programming language offers.

i) character

Characters are single literal expressions that can be used in a program. They are usually used to input responses from the user while running the program. Characters occupy very less memory storage and are considered good for the allocation of program resources.

%c is usually used to designate the output of characters in the programming languages.

ii) Strings

Strings are the advanced implementation of character expressions. In the real world, it is not feasible to just use characters for expressing entities. Strings are one of the often-used data types while developing computer programs.

%s is usually used to designate strings in the programming languages.

c) Boolean data types

Programming is a logical process where the computer should often decide between the choices that are given to it. Sometimes they may be random but they are usually followed by a logical equivalence. All the conditional and loop statements depend on Boolean data types.

Usually, there are only two Boolean data types that are true and false.

There are defined by the identifier _Bool. Bool variables can change the understanding of the program execution process.

Here is an example:

if (x >3)

{

  _Bool = true;

   printf(" Enter the condition here")

}

In the above example of a C program, the program is executed only when the logical statement is true. If it doesn't satisfy the logical statement then the program will end and give compilation errors.

Boolean data types are essential for a lot of logical programs and software.

With this, we have completed a brief explanation about variables and data types.

Variable declaration and assignment can be thoroughly understood only when you practice coding a lot of programs.

We recommend you to look at different open source projects to understand the importance of variables. In the next chapter, we will learn about pointers in depth.

Follow along!

Chapter 14: Pointers

```
int add_array (int *a, int num_elements);  ⟩─ ①
int main() {
  int Tab[5] = {100, 220, 37, 16, 98};
  printf("Total summation is %d\n", add_array(Tab, 5));   ⟩ ②
  return 0;}
int add_array (int *p, int size) {
  int total = 0;
  int k;
  for (k = 0; k < size; k++) {           ⟩─ ①
    total += p[k];  |
  return (total);;}
```

This chapter is a clear introduction to one of the most controversial and most discussed features of C language that is pointers. No other programming languages provide pointers as a feature in their index.

The extremely low-level interaction with the hardware resources is one of the reasons why pointers have become a reality in the C programming language.

In this chapter, we will give a short introduction to pointers with several examples.

Follow along to know more about it.

What are the pointers?

First of all, to understand the concept of pointers we need to let you understand the process of indirection in computing and in real life. Let us imagine that you are the manager of a book store.

A customer approaches you and asks for a book that is not available in the book store. So, what will you do next? You will inform the wholesale book supplier to get the book for your customer.

That wholesale supplier you contacted will reach out to other book suppliers to give it to you.

So, if you look at this example carefully you 'the manager' just acted as a medium to deliver the book for your customer. You did not directly go to the book supplier to get that desired book.

This process of mediating things to complete a task is known as indirection. Pointers in C follows the same mechanism. They provide access to the data value you are searching for.

Just like how indirection reduces cost fares for the manager of the book store, pointers help programmers to strategically manage resources.

In the next section, we will in detail discuss declaring a pointer with examples. Follow along!

How to declare pointers?

First of all, you need to create a variable that can be used to declare pointer variables.

Here is the variable:

int sample = 34;

As soon as you declare a variable it is declared a storage location in the system. You can check it using the ampersand symbol '&'.

For example:

&sample;

Output:

0dfd656

The memory location will always be in a hexadecimal format.

In the next section, you need to declare a variable that can act as a pointer.

All you need to do is add an asterisk in front of the identifier name to declare it as a pointer.

Here is the format:

int *data_pointer

The above statement roughly states that a pointer of an integer data type with the name data_pointer is created. After the pointer is declared you can use it to point out to other variables.

In the next step, we will use this pointer to store the first variable location that we have created. This will make you understand the importance of pointers in memory allocation statements.

Here is the format:

data_pointer = &sample

Now, whenever you call the pointer, you will get the output as the storage location of the sample variable.

Output:

0dfd656

You can also use an asterisk as an indirection operator to denote all the variables that a pointer holds.

Here is the format:

*data_pointer

Output:

sample

With this, we have completed a brief explanation about the declaration about the pointers.

In the next section, we will in detail discuss some of the advantages that pointers possess in the C programming language.

Follow along!

Advantages of pointers

1) With the help of pointers, you can create a more optimized code. For example, if you use static buffers to enclose a large list of values instead of pointers, they may lead to buffer flow errors. However, with the usage of pointers, memory allocation works perfectly and makes you create more complex programs.

2) Pointers are an essential component that needs to be used while dealing with multidimensional arrays that hold a lot of elements. Pointers are also extensively used to create data structures such as heaps, graphs, and trees.

3) Dynamic memory allocation is very essential if you have fewer computing resources. Pointers are the only way to maintain an equilibrium between the resources available. If not of pointers, C programming language will become clumsy and may need to deal with a lot of run-time errors before starting the execution of the program.

4) They are very useful when you are trying to do repetitive tasks such as refreshing an element or for sorting algorithms.

Null pointers

Null pointers are a special type of pointers where they are pointed out to a null value. Null pointers are used when they are not allowed to produce any return values.

Here is an example:

int *pointer = NULL;

Now, whenever you call the pointer in a function you will get a null value as a result.

How to use pointers in Functions?

Pointers and functions can be used cumulatively to produce results. Pointers can use functions as return statements and values. Whereas, functions can also use points as their function parameters and arguments.

Here is how you can use a pointer as a function argument:

functionname(data_pointer)

When the logical equivalence statements are written they take the data_pointer argument as a pointer.

You can use this argument in the function body as:

void main()

{

  functionname int *data_point;

}

When the pointer is called it displays the storage location as the output result.

Remember that by changing the function arguments using a pointer you can change the instances of the pointer but you cannot change the actual storage location of the variable that you are dealing with.

Pointers along with functions can be used for faster results in software.

Using this method, you can easily exchange values between two variables.

Here is the program:

```
main()
{
  variable1 = data_pointer
   varaible2 = *data_pointer
   result = &variable2
   varaiabe2 = *varaible1
}
```

When the results are produced you will find out that the values of the variables have been exchanged.

How to use pointers for arrays?

Arrays can also use pointers to deal with complex multi-dimensional operations. They are used in both one-dimensional and two-dimensional arrays.

Here is a program:

```
main()
{
  int variable[] = data_pointer

  &varaible[] = *data_pointer

  *data_pointer = int variable[]
}
```

In the above program, pointers are pointed out to arrays. They are very useful if you are dealing with a huge chunk of data.

With this, we have completed a brief introduction to pointers.

In the next chapter, we will with examples give a brief description of double pointers.

Follow along to know more about it in detail.

Chapter 15: Dual pointers

In the previous chapter, we have discussed pointers in detail. We have given you various examples to help you understand the impact of pointers in C programming.

This chapter introduces a double pointer (also called as Pointer to Pointer) in short with few examples.

Follow along to understand about double pointers.

Let us go!

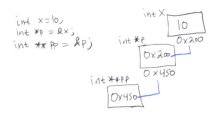

What is a double pointer?

As discussed in the previous chapter pointers usually point out to the variable location they are assigned to and they are represented by an asterisk (*). Double pointers are a little bit advanced way to store address values.

When a double pointer is created it is designed in a way such that it can store the location value of the first pointer that is been assigned with storage value.

The double-pointer is represented with a double asterisk (**). You can further continue this concept with three, four and an infinite pointer to pointer sequences.

Declaring a double-pointer

Declaring double pointers are quite similar to the declaration of pointers.

All you need to do is add an extra asterisk alongside it. This is similar if you are implementing it in arrays or in structures.

Here is the format:

string **ptr;

// A double pointer is created

Understanding Double pointers

In this section, we will help you understand double pointers in-depth with the help of an example below.

Here is the program code:

```
#include {Enter the libraries here}
// This is an example for double pointer
int main()
{
    string value = "Gold";
  // Now we will create a pointer
    int *create;
  // Now we will create a double-pointer
    int **double;
  // Now will display the storage value
    create = &value;
  // Now will display the storage of pointer
    double = &create;
  // We will just print out the result
    printf("Value of the variable = %d\n", var );
    printf(" Let us display pointer entity = %f\n", *create );
    printf(" Let us display double pointer = %f\n", **double);
  }
```

Output:

Value of variable = GOLD

Pointer entity: 2s737

Double pointer entity: 0x776

When you look at the programming code, you will understand how double pointers are created.

In the next chapter, we will learn about creating a C program using an IDE.

Follow along!

Chapter 16: Creating a C program

In the previous chapters of this book, you have learned about various components that make up an effective program.

This chapter is a brief one that explains you a step by step instruction to create a C program in an integrated development environment.

This short chapter will let you understand the basic process of the C programming procedure.

How to create a C program?

Step 1:

First of all, you need to download your favorable IDE from the official website. In this chapter, we will use the NetBeans IDE to run the C program that we are going to create.

Step 2:

After installing the NetBeans IDE open it from the menu and create a new C file from the create menu in the bottom tray of the system. Make sure the extension of the file is .C. If not, the program will not get compiled by the IDE

Step 3:

Now, enter the given program in the IDE

// Program to check whether a number is even or odd

#include<stdio.h>

// This is called a pre processing library

void main()

{

   int sample = 6;

   if(sample /2)

   printf(" This is an even number');

   else

   print(" This is an odd number');

}

Step 4:

After entering the following C program in the IDE save it from the options on the menu. After saving it you are now already to compile it in the NetBeans IDE. Use the compile button from the menu. You can use F3 to compile.

Step 5:

The compilation procedure will start and will show success if there are no errors. However, if there are any errors in the program they will be shown up in sequential order.

Step 6:

After compiling and if there are no errors you can click the Run (F5) button to display the output. You can also debug the code while it is running.

This is the normal procedure to create, compile and run a C program in an IDE.

In the next chapter, we will discuss dealing with errors in detail.

Let us go!

Chapter 17: Common errors in C programming

In the previous chapters of this book, we have discussed various components and lexical syntax that can help us create an effective programming code.

That particular effective program is then compiled to run in any operating system. However, the compiler will check the whole programming code and decide whether it is good by itself to run or not.

If there are any errors related to syntax, function or run-time the program will terminate immediately and show the reasons for the error.

As a programmer, it is an essential skill to have sufficient information about the types of errors you are going to deal with.

If you can't understand the complexity of error you have encountered then it is very difficult to create effective code. So, to make you aware of the essential information of the types of errors available in C language we provided this chapter.

Learn carefully and try to use google if you ever face any error.

Clearing errors is the best way to learn to program.

Let us go!

What is an error?

Usually, programs expect a certain numerical, analytical or logical result to the program they have compiled. If you are unable to get the desired result for your program then it is called an error. Remember that a bug is not an error.

A bug is a programmatical mistake that will let exploiters take advantage of it. Usually, bad programming principles cause an error.

Errors are made by programmers because of a mistake in syntax or because of not following basic programming rules of that particular language.

For example, you can't use reserved keywords as a variable in C programming language, So, if you use 'for' keyword in a variable then it will show you a syntax error. [for is a reserved keyword]

Errors in C

C programming language is famously known for its unique way of representing error syntaxes in the output results. Unlike other high-level programming languages, C is said to be strict with case sensitive letters and whitespaces.

It is naturally a difficult language to learn because it strictly follows all the guidelines.

In this section, we will in detail explain the different errors that are available in C programming language.

Follow along!

a) Syntax error

The syntax is like grammar to a programming language. Without exact precise statements, the compiler will not allow you to proceed further.

In layman terms, syntax errors appear in C language when there is a mistake related to the syntax of the program. For example, wrong variable names and data types can cause syntax errors.

Different programming languages use different syntax rules. So, if you are new to any programming language, we suggest you learn in-depth about different syntactical rules that the language uses. It is often easy to debug syntax errors because the compiler shows the exact code line for you.

All you need to do is use the correct syntax in the place of incorrect syntax to make the program work.

Here is an example:

int a= 5.7493;

Output:

Syntax error. You can't proceed further

The above example ended up with a syntax error because the variable is declared as an int data type value but is given a floating-point literal.

b) Runtime errors

Runtime errors appear when a programmer does a mistake in the program operations that needs to be committed. In simple terms, runtime errors appear when the errors are related to the technical analysis of the program.

For example, if you call a function that is not yet created it gives a run time error. Run time errors are a little bit difficult to clear off because of the ambiguity they possess.

Some of the example of run time errors:

1) Making bad and undefined calculations is a classic use case. For example, dividing a number by zero is a good way to understand it. When you divide any number by zero it is of undefined format. A computer doesn't know how to represent or output the result that doesn't exist. So, it displays runtime errors during the compilation process.

2) A lot of file management operations often end up with run time errors. For example, opening a file that is not yet even created is not possible. So, an ambiguity is created and a run time error will be displayed.

3) A lot of complex programs also face run time errors when all the memory is allocated to the program. For example, buffer overflows can cause a run time error.

Here is an example:

int a=3;

a/0;

Output:

Runtime error -- You cannot divide a variable with zero

c)Logical error

Programming is a lexical language that uses different identifiers and literals to complete tasks with a computer. Programming logics are incomplete without logical statements and expressions. For example, OR AND NOT all are considered as logical operators that can be used to compare expressions and statements.

Logical equivalence statements are also often prone to errors due to the ambiguity they create in the programming languages.

Logical errors are often difficult to notice because they will not completely stop the compilation process but will give faulty results. They are like machine learning applications to say in layman terms.

Here is an example:

int a=+b;

Here an unnecessary assignment operator is used resulting in faulty execution of the program.

Warnings in C programming

Warnings are different from errors in the programming language. Warnings will not stop the execution of the program. They act as signals that inform you about the ineffectiveness of the program.

Compilers suspect that the code you have written is not good in terms of execution. So, when you detect a warning while executing the written code, we suggest you make some changes and re-execute it.

Here is an example:

Warning -- This may need more resources

With this, we have completed a brief explanation about errors and warnings in the C programming language.

As said before, even experienced programmers face errors while dealing with programming code. So, always make sure that you feel challenging whenever you see a programming error.

Before ending this book, here are some tips to improve your C programming skills exponentially:

1) Register yourself with GitHub and start reading various open-source code available. Good code can be written only when you are aware of the good code that has been written already.

2) Start contributing to open-source projects. Always start with simple projects and extend your skills by involving complex projects with a lot of contributors.

3) Don't feel low when you face errors. Clear your doubts with the help of forums such as Stack Overflow.

With this, we have completed a brief explanation about errors in this chapter and thus we are in the end parts of our book.

We have discussed a good number of topics related to C programming in this book.

All the best!

Conclusion

Glad that you have reached the end of this book. I hope you have enjoyed the content provided in the book as much we loved making this book.

What to do next?

As you have completed a complex and thorough book that deals with C programming it is now a huge test for you to apply your programming skills on real time projects. There are a lot of open-source projects that are waiting for a contribution. Remember that reading a lot of C language code will also help you understand the programming logics that C possesses.

That's it! Thanks for purchasing this book again and All the best!

"Did this book help you in some way? If so, I'd love to hear about it.

Honest reviews help readers find the right book for their needs."

www.ingramcontent.com/pod-product-compliance
Lightning Source LLC
Chambersburg PA
CBHW041151050326
40690CB00001B/434